# JOYFUL FIGHTER

**JOURNAL FOR TEENS**

*A JOURNAL TO WRITE ABOUT YOUR DAY, YOUR FEELINGS, OR JUST TO RELAX AND DISTRACT YOURSELF FROM THE DAY-TO-DAY.*

## DIANE BEYER

ISBN: 978-1-960136-44-2

Here is a journal to help you through your hospital stay. There are daily log pages for you to keep track of how you felt, your goals, who came to see you, and more. Remember to always find joy in your day. Even when the days are hard there is always something to be joyful about. There is a list of positive affirmations to help remind you to be strong. You will find writing prompts, activities, and coloring pages. Let this journal be your steadfast companion, guiding you through each day with positivity and purpose, reminding you that strength and joy can be found in every moment, no matter how challenging.

# Affirmations

**Here are some affirmations that you might find helpful:**

Remember, affirmations can be a powerful tool for staying positive and hopeful during challenging times. Choose the affirmations that resonate most with you and repeat them to yourself regularly

1. My body is strong and capable of healing.

2. I am surrounded by people who care about me and do everything they can to help me feel better.

3. Each day brings me closer to full recovery.

4. I am brave and resilient in the face of adversity.

5. My mind is powerful and can help me stay positive and hopeful.

6. I am grateful for the opportunity to rest and allow my body to heal.

7. I am not alone in this experience, and there are many other people who have gone through similar situations.

8. My strength and determination will help me get through this difficult time.

9. I trust my medical team and know they are doing everything they can to help me get better.

10. This experience will make me stronger and more appreciative of my health in the future.

# Create a Bucket List

A bucket list is a list of things you want to do, places you want to go, and experiences you want to have. It's a way to keep track of all the things you want to do in your life and to help you stay focused on achieving your goals.

To create a bucket list, start by thinking about the things you're most interested in or passionate about. What are some activities or experiences that you've always dreamed of doing? Do you want to travel to a specific place, learn a new skill, or try a particular food?

Write down all of your ideas, no matter how big or small they may seem. Then, prioritize the items on your list and figure out which ones you want to accomplish first. You can also break down larger goals into smaller steps to make them more manageable.

Remember, a bucket list isn't set in stone. You can add to it or modify it as you grow and experience new things. The important thing is to have fun and make the most of your life!

# Dream Big Bucket List

_____

_____

_____

_____

_____

_____

_____

_____

Today's Joy

Date.............. HOW AM I FEELING?

| At wake up | At Bedtime |
|---|---|
| | |

Goals for Today

What's on my mind?

Activities

Visitors

ARE THERE ANY SPECIFIC
RITUALS, MANTRAS, OR
INSPIRATIONAL QUOTES THAT
GIVE YOU STRENGTH AND
MOTIVATION?

"Believe in yourself and all that you are. Know that there is something inside you
that is greater than any obstacle."
Christian D. Larson

# TIC TAC TOE

**Player 2:**

**Player 1:**

Today's Joy

Date..............

HOW AM I FEELING?

| At wake up | At Bedtime |
|---|---|
| | |

Goals for Today

What's on my mind?

Activities

Visitors

What if you could have any pet in the hospital?
What would you want?

"Your current situation is not your final destination."
Unknown

Today's Joy

Date..............

HOW AM I FEELING?

| At wake up | At Bedtime |
|---|---|
|  |  |

Goals for Today

What's on my mind?

Activities

Visitors

Are there any treatments that you enjoy or dislike?

_____

_____

_____

_____

_____

_____

_____

_____

_____

_____

_____

"You are stronger than you think, and this too shall pass."
Unknown

Today's Joy

Date..............

**HOW AM I FEELING?**

| At wake up | At Bedtime |
| --- | --- |
| | |

Goals for Today

What's on my mind?

Activities

Visitors

Write about the first item on your
bucket list.

# WOULD YOU RATHER...

HAVE THE ABILITY TO FLY

**OR**

BE ABLE TO BREATHE UNDERWATER LIKE A FISH

HAVE THE POWER TO CONTROL FIRE

**OR**

HAVE THE POWER TO CONTROL THE WEATHER

BE ABLE TO SPEAK & UNDERSTAND EVERY LANGUAGE IN THE WORLD

HAVE THE TALENT TO PLAY ANY MUSICAL INSTRUMENT

HAVE THE POWER TO TELEPORT ANYWHERE INSTANTLY

**OR**

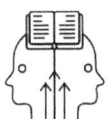

HAVE THE ABILITY TO READ MINDS

Today's Joy

Date.............

HOW AM I FEELING?

| At wake up | At Bedtime |
| --- | --- |
|  |  |

Goals for Today

What's on my mind?

Activities

Visitors

Describe your daily routine. What
is your favorite part of the day?

"The only way to get through it is to go through it."
Unknown

Today's Joy

Date..............

HOW AM I FEELING?

| At wake up | At Bedtime |
|---|---|
| | |

Goals for Today

What's on my mind?

Activities

Visitors

What if you could have any wish
granted to make your stay better?
What would you wish for?

_____

_____

_____

_____

_____

_____

_____

_____

_____

_____

_____

_____

_____

_____

"The harder you fall, the higher you bounce."
Unknown

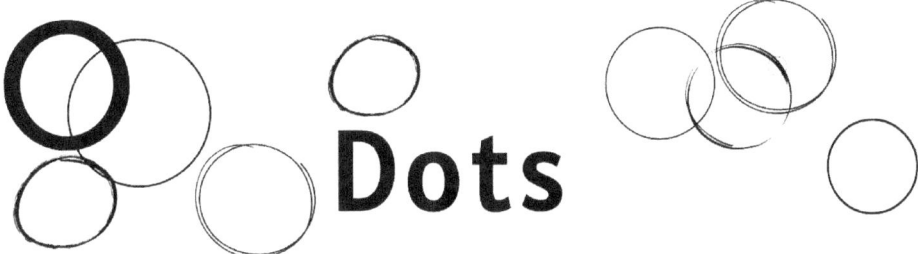

# Dots

Dots is a fun game where each player takes a turn connecting one dot to another adjacent dot either horizontally or vertically. Each player takes one move at a time drawing a line. Eventually the board starts to fill with lines. Some will be connected and some not. When you can add a final line to forms a square, fill in the box with your initial and take another turn. The objective is to have the most boxes with your initials.

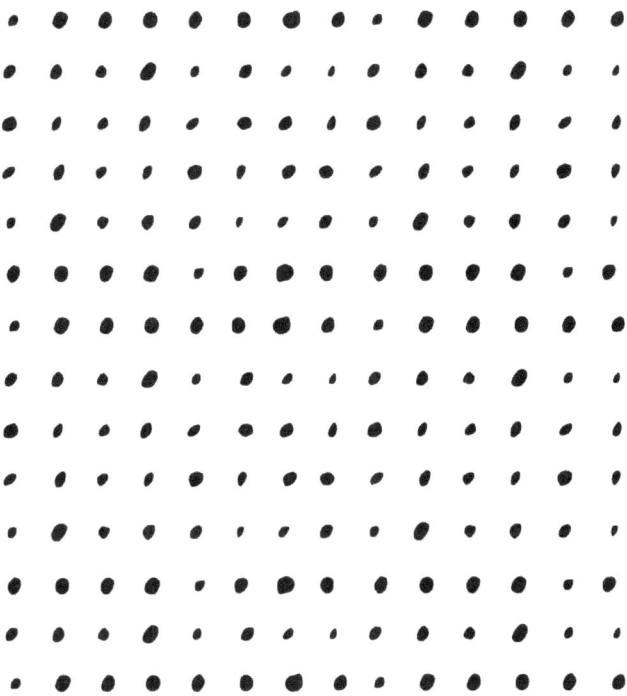

**Today's Joy**

Date..............

HOW AM I FEELING?

| At wake up | At Bedtime |
|---|---|
| | |

**Goals for Today**

**What's on my mind?**

**Activities**

Visitors

Do you have any strategies to
help you stay positive?

"Every day may not be good, but there is something good in every day."
Alice Morse Earle

Date..............

**Today's Joy**

**HOW AM I FEELING?**

| At wake up | At Bedtime |
|---|---|
| | |

**Goals for Today**

**What's on my mind?**

**Activities**

Visitors

What are some challenges you are
facing during your stay?

"Storms make trees take deeper roots."
Dolly Parton

Unscramble the positive words below

VELO                    _____

PNIHSAEPS               _____

IESLM                   _____

DSISKENN                _____

TRUDTGEAI               _____

EOPH                    _____

RNVCEEEESRAP            _____

LEBEVEI                 _____

CEPEA                   _____

RLMECIA                 _____

MUHTPRI                 _____

GCREANEOU               _____

TGUARLEH                _____

CJEIREO                 _____

FAUGRLET                _____

# JOYFUL
## WORD SCRAMBLE

Answer Key

**LOVE**

**HAPPINESS**

**SMILE**

**KINDNESS**

**GRADTITUDE**

**HOPE**

**PERSEVERANCE**

**BELIEVE**

**PEACE**

**MIRACLE**

**TRIUMPH**

**ENCOURAGE**

**LAUGHTER**

**REJOICE**

**GRATEFUL**

Today's Joy

Date..............

HOW AM I FEELING?

| At wake up | At Bedtime |
| --- | --- |
| | |

Goals for Today

What's on my mind?

Activities

Visitors

How are you trying to find
strength and courage to
overcome your fears?

"Difficult roads often lead to beautiful destinations."
Zig Ziglar

**Today's Joy**

Date..............

**HOW AM I FEELING?**

| At wake up | At Bedtime |
|---|---|
| | |

**Goals for Today**

**What's on my mind?**

**Activities**

# Visitors

# What are you grateful for during your hospital stay?

"You never know how strong you are until being strong is the only choice you have."
Bob Marley

Today's Joy

Date..............

HOW AM I FEELING?

| At wake up | At Bedtime |
|---|---|
|  |  |

Goals for Today

What's on my mind?

Activities

Visitors

What if you could design your
own hospital room? What would
it look like?

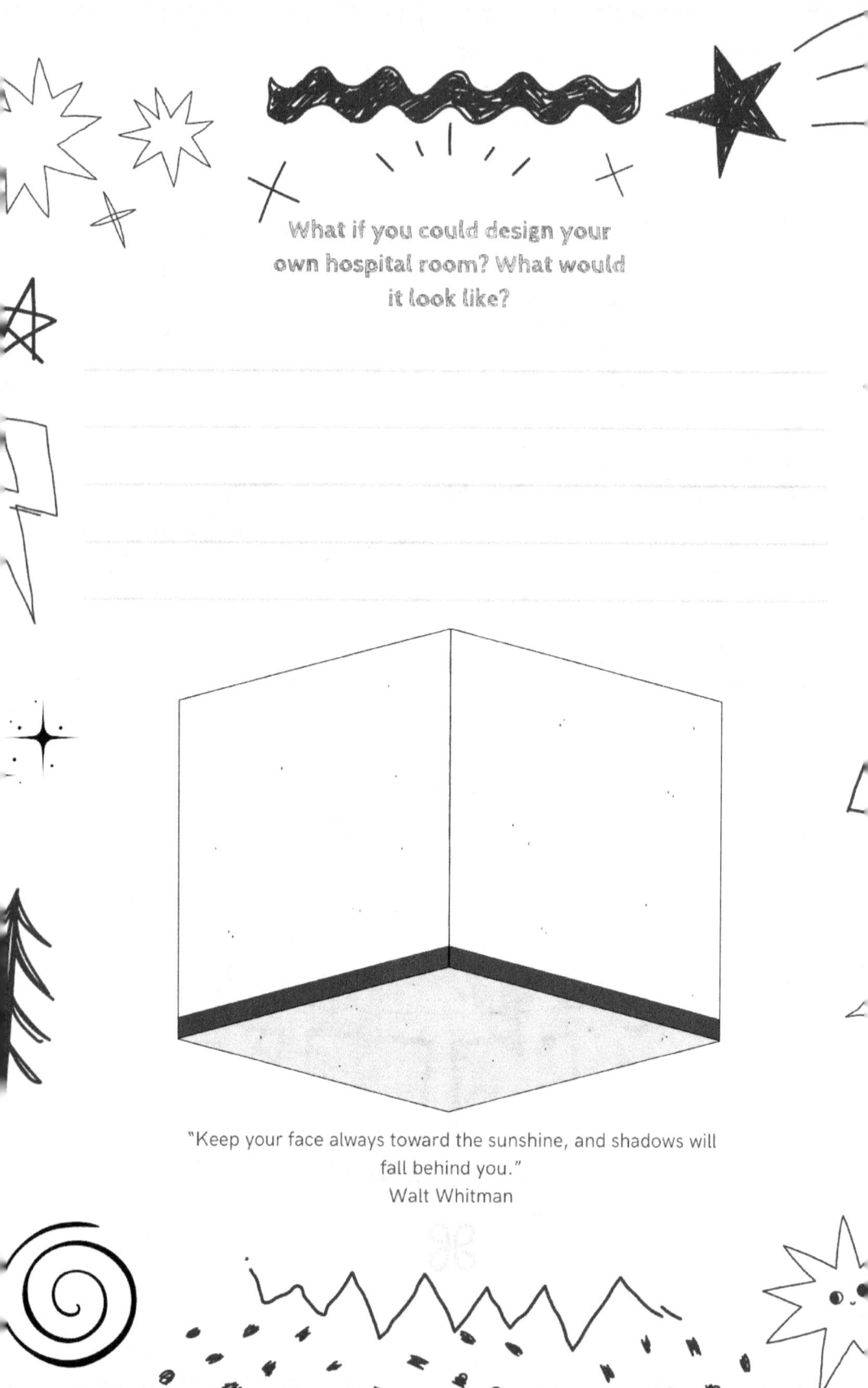

"Keep your face always toward the sunshine, and shadows will
fall behind you."
Walt Whitman

# THE CIRCLE CHALLENGE

Directions: What are you able to make out of a circle? You have 3 minutes to turn as many circles as you can into an object

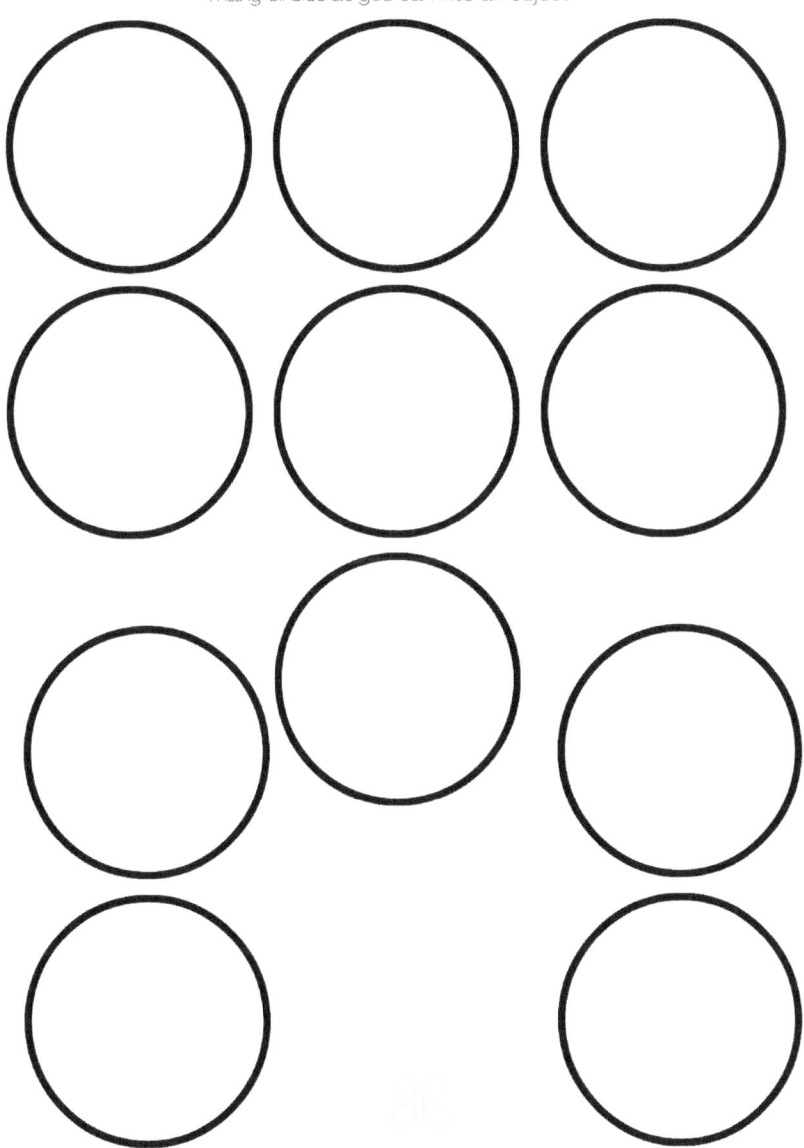

Today's Joy

Date...............

HOW AM I FEELING?

| At wake up | At Bedtime |
|---|---|
| | |

Goals for Today

What's on my mind?

Activities

Visitors

Share a memorable interaction
that made you feel supported and
encouraged.

"You are not alone in this. You are loved and supported."
Unknown

Today's Joy

Date...............

HOW AM I FEELING?

| At wake up | At Bedtime |
|---|---|
|  |  |

Goals for Today

What's on my mind?

Activities

Visitors

What if you could have any nurse or doctor take care of you during your hospital stay? Who would you choose?

"You are braver than you believe, stronger than you seem, and smarter than you think."
A.A Milne

**Today's Joy**

Date..............

**HOW AM I FEELING?**

| At wake up | At Bedtime |
|---|---|
| | |

**Goals for Today**

**What's on my mind?**

**Activities**

Visitors

What do you appreciate the most
about people visiting you?

"Life is tough, my darling, but so are you."
Stephanie Bennett-Henry

# MY Hospital Comic

Today's Joy

Date...............

HOW AM I FEELING?

| At wake up | At Bedtime |
|---|---|
| | |

Goals for Today

What's on my mind?

Activities

Visitors

What specific activities, exercises, or mindfulness practices help you feel grounded and calm?

_____

_____

_____

_____

_____

_____

_____

_____

_____

_____

"You are not defined by your circumstances, but by how you react to them."
Unknown

**Today's Joy**

Date...............

**HOW AM I FEELING?**

| At wake up | At Bedtime |
| --- | --- |
|  |  |

**Goals for Today**

**What's on my mind?**

**Activities**

**Visitors**

Write about a dream destination on your bucket list.

_____

_____

_____

_____

_____

_____

_____

_____

_____

_____

_____

_____

_____

_____

_____

_____

*"You are capable of withstanding anything that comes your way."*
Unknown

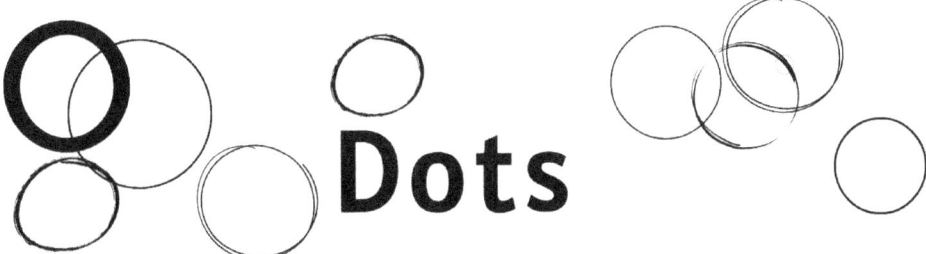

# Dots

Dots is a fun game where each player takes a turn connecting one dot to another adjacent dot either horizontally or vertically. Each player takes one move at a time drawing a line. Eventually the board starts to fill with lines. Some will be connected and some not. When you can add a final line to forms a square, fill in the box with your initial and take another turn. The objective is to have the most boxes with your initials.

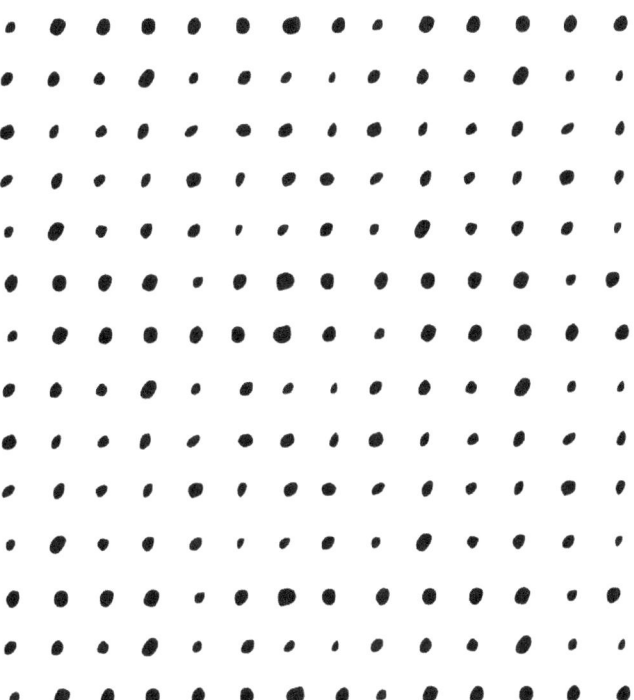

Today's Joy

Date.............. HOW AM I FEELING?

| At wake up | At Bedtime |
|---|---|
| | |

Goals for Today

What's on my mind?

Activities

Visitors

What brings you comfort in the hospital?

"Courage is not the absence of fear, but the triumph over it."
Nelson Mandela

Today's Joy

Date..............

**HOW AM I FEELING?**

| At wake up | At Bedtime |
|------------|------------|
|            |            |

Goals for Today

What's on my mind?

Activities

Visitors

What if you could have any visitor come to see you?
Who would you choose?

"Strength doesn't come from what you can do. It comes from
overcoming the things you once thought you couldn't."
Rikki Rogers

# TIC TAC TOE

**Player 2:**

**Player 1:**

Today's Joy

Date..............

HOW AM I FEELING?

| At woke up | At Bedtime |
|---|---|
|  |  |

Goals for Today

What's on my mind?

Activities

Visitors

Write a letter to your future self expressing your hopes
and dreams for the person you will become.

"Your present circumstances don't determine where you
can go; they merely determine where you start."
Nido Qubein

(

Today's Joy

Date..............

HOW AM I FEELING?

| At wake up | At Bedtime |
|---|---|
|  |  |

Goals for Today

What's on my mind?

Activities

Visitors

Are your family and friends visiting often?
How do their visits and calls make you feel?

"The struggles you're facing today develop the strength you need for tomorrow."
Unknown

CREATE YOUR
OWN EMOJIS

Today's Joy

Date..............

**HOW AM I FEELING?**

| At wake up | At Bedtime |
| --- | --- |
| | |

Goals for Today

What's on my mind?

Activities

Visitors

Who are some people who inspire you?

"Life doesn't get easier or more forgiving, we get stronger and more resilient."
Steve Maraboli

**Today's Joy**

Date..............

HOW AM I FEELING?

| At wake up | At Bedtime |
|---|---|

**Goals for Today**

**What's on my mind?**

**Activities**

Visitors

Are there any activities or gestures people have done to make you feel connected and cared for?

"When everything seems to be going against you, remember that the airplane takes off against the wind, not with it."
Henry Ford

# WOULD YOU RATHER...

 **OR**

HAVE THE ABILITY TO BECOME INVISIBLE

HAVE SUPER STRENGTH

 **OR**

LIVE IN A WORLD WITHOUT INTERNET

LIVE IN A WORLD WITHOUT SMARTPHONES

 **OR**

BE ABLE TO TIME TRAVEL TO THE PAST

TIME TRAVEL TO THE FUTURE

 **OR**

HAVE THE POWER TO HEAL ANY ILLNESS

HAVE THE POWER TO BRING HAPPINESS TO ANYONE YOU MEET

Today's Joy

Date..............

HOW AM I FEELING?

| At wake up | At Bedtime |
| --- | --- |
| | |

Goals for Today

What's on my mind?

Activities

Visitors

Do you have any fears or worries about your health in the future?

_____

_____

_____

_____

_____

_____

_____

_____

_____

_____

_____

_____

_____

_____

"When we welcome miracles in our life anything is possible."
Dr. Beth Creel

Today's Joy

Date..............

HOW AM I FEELING?

| At wake up | At Bedtime |
|---|---|
|  |  |

Goals for Today

What's on my mind?

Activities

Visitors

Reflect on the people you have met in the hospital.

"The world breaks us all, and afterward some are stronger in those broken places."
Ernest Hemingway

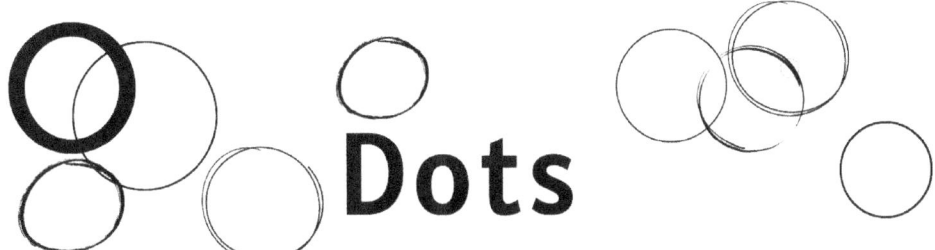

# Dots

Dots is a fun game where each player takes a turn connecting one dot to another adjacent dot either horizontally or vertically. Each player takes one move at a time drawing a line. Eventually the board starts to fill with lines. Some will be connected and some not. When you can add a final line to forms a square, fill in the box with your initial and take another turn. The objective is to have the most boxes with your initials.

Today's Joy

Date..............

HOW AM I FEELING?

| At wake up | At Bedtime |
|------------|------------|
|            |            |

Goals for Today

What's on my mind?

Activities

Visitors

Are you dealing with any physical or emotional difficulties?
How are you coping with them?

"Strength does not come from physical capacity. It comes from an indomitable will."
Mahatma Gandhi

Today's Joy

Date.............. HOW AM I FEELING?

| At wake up | At Bedtime |
|---|---|
|  |  |

Goals for Today

What's on my mind?

Activities

Visitors

Describe any creative outlets or hobbies you've explored while in the hospital.

_____

_____

_____

_____

_____

_____

_____

_____

_____

_____

_____

"There is no greater gift that you can give yourself than attention."
Dr. Beth Creel

What if you could change one thing about the world? What would you change, and how do you think it would impact society?

_____

_____

_____

_____

_____

_____

_____

_____

Today's Joy

Date..............

HOW AM I FEELING?

| At wake up | At Bedtime |
|---|---|

Goals for Today

What's on my mind?

Activities

Visitors

What if you could have any meal or snack delivered to your room? What would you have?

"You are stronger than the storm."
Unknown

Today's Joy

Date..............

HOW AM I FEELING?

| At wake up | At Bedtime |
|---|---|
| | |

Goals for Today

What's on my mind?

Activities

Visitors

What lessons do you think you will learn from your time
in the hospital?

_____

_____

_____

_____

_____

_____

_____

_____

_____

_____

_____

"Whoever survives the test must tell his story. That is his duty."
Elie Wiesel

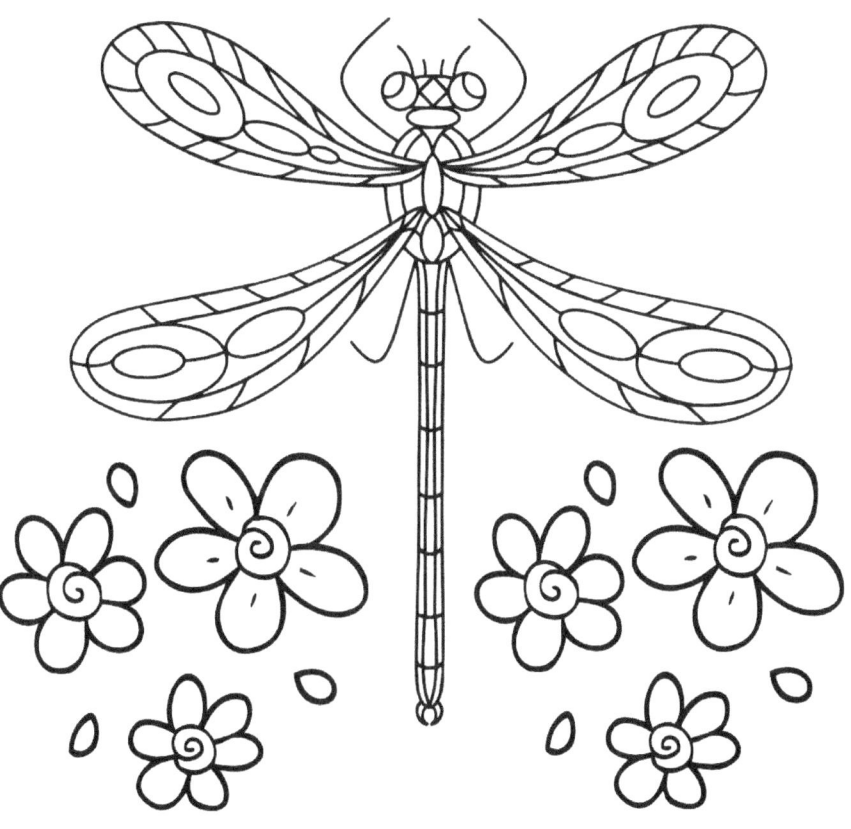

Today's Joy

Date..............

HOW AM I FEELING?

| At wake up | At Bedtime |
|---|---|
|  |  |

Goals for Today

What's on my mind?

Activities

Visitors

What are you looking forward to when you get better?

"Turning toward what you deeply love saves you."
Rumi

Date..............

**Today's Joy**

**HOW AM I FEELING?**

| At wake up | At Bedtime |
| --- | --- |
| | |

**Goals for Today**

**What's on my mind?**

**Activities**

Visitors

WHAT WERE YOUR INITIAL
EMOTIONS WHEN YOU FIRST
ARRIVED AT THE HOSPITAL?

"The human spirit is stronger than anything that can happen to it."
C.C. Scott

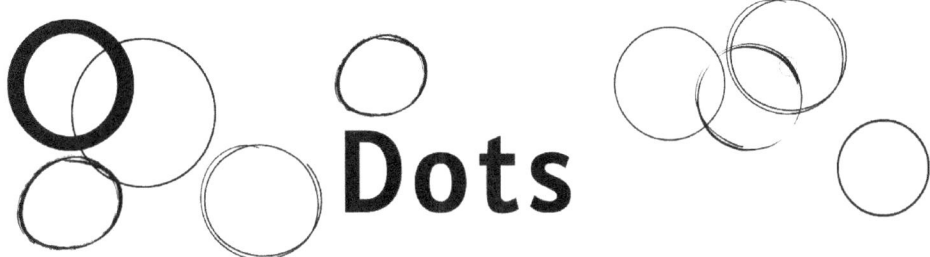

# Dots

Dots is a fun game where each player takes a turn connecting one dot to another adjacent dot either horizontally or vertically. Each player takes one move at a time drawing a line. Eventually the board starts to fill with lines. Some will be connected and some not. When you can add a final line to forms a square, fill in the box with your initial and take another turn. The objective is to have the most boxes with your initials.

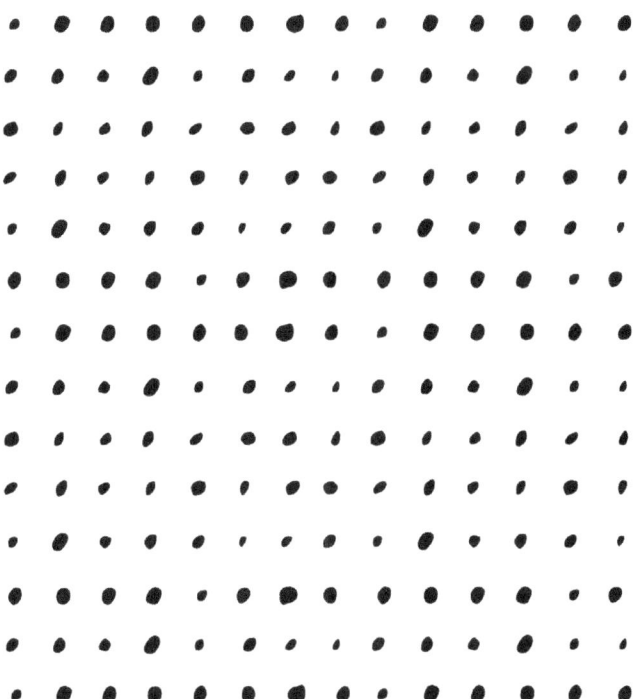

I hope this journal has helped you remember that there is joy in every day.

Our mission at Joyful Fighter is to bring joy, comfort, and organization to children with medical needs and those who love them. We strive to help families have an easier time with hospital life. We have been there too and understand the struggles you are facing. There are lots of resources out there.

## Please visit
## Joyfulfighter.com

to check out our other products and helpful resources.

# About the Author

My name is Diane Beyer. I am a hard-working single mother. I moved to Las Vegas from the east coast in 2004 and have worked as a cook and a chef at a few hotels. Growing up, I saw my mother fight complications from diabetes and heart disease. My mother lost her battle when I was 20 years old. This not only made me strong, but helped prepare me for the journey I would take 12 years later. My daughter Candice was born with a severe heart condition, lung problems and blood disorders. She passed away at two and a half years old. I have made it my mission and Candice's legacy to help families going through medically challenging times. I wrote and published a hospital journal to help caregivers stay positive, focused, and organized while in the hospital. I also started Joyful Fighter Fashion in 2016, a business making fashionable hospital gowns for children.

When your child is in the hospital, as a parent you may feel scared, sad, and helpless. I want to help change those feelings to strength, joy, and hope.

Sometimes you need to adjust your environment to feel better. You can bring some joy and fun into your room by playing dress up. Who doesn't feel better when you put on something pretty?

My gowns help you feel like you have some control. As a parent of a special needs child, you understand how the little things can make a big difference.

www.ingramcontent.com/pod-product-compliance
Lightning Source LLC
Chambersburg PA
CBHW071011120626
46546CB00003B/1037